21ST
CENTURY
DEBATES

GENETICS

THE IMPACT ON OUR LIVES

PAUL DOWSWELL

HODDER
Wayland

an imprint of Hodder Children's Books

21st Century Debates Series

Climate Change
Endangered Species
Energy
Genetics
Internet
Media
Population Explosion
Rainforests
Surveillance
Waste and Recycling

Produced for Hodder Wayland by Discovery Books Limited, Unit 3, 37 Watling Street, Leintwardine, Shropshire SY7 0LW, England.

Editor: Patience Coster
Series editor: Alex Woolf
Series design: Mind's Eye Design, Lewes
Artwork: Stefan Chabluk, Christopher Halls

First published in 2000 by Hodder Wayland, an imprint of Hodder Children's Books, 338 Euston Road, London NW1 3BH, England.

British Library Cataloguing in Publication Data

ISBN 0 7502 2768 0

Printed and bound in Italy by G.Canale & C.S.p.A., Turin.

Picture acknowledgements: Bettmann/Corbis 26; Bruce Coleman Collection 22 (Alain Compost); Corbis 28 (Peter Turnley); Natural History Photographic Agency 17, 23 (Anthony Bannister); Popperfoto 9, 27; Popperfoto/Reuter 14, 15, 25, 44, 50; Proctor & Gamble 42; Royal Free Hospital School of Medicine/Wellcome Trust Photo Library 45; Science Photo Library 5 (Ken Eward), 8 (US Navy), 10, 13 (Chris Knapton), 18 (Ed Young/Agstock), 21 (Hank Morgan), 32 (Philippe Plailly), 33 (J C Revy), 34 (James King-Holmes), 35 (Hank Morgan), 36 (J C Revy), 37 (David Parker), 38, 39 (Philippe Plailly), 47 (Chris Priest), 48 (Saturn Stills), 54 James King-Holmes, 55 (Victor Habbick Visions), 56 (Klaus Guldbrandsen), 57 (Victor Habbick Visions), 58 (Catherine Pouedras/Eurelios), 59 (Dr Jeremy Burgess); Tony Stone Images 6 (Lori Adamski Peek), 31 (Charles Thatcher), 40 (Fernand Ivaldi), 43, 46 (D E Cox), 53 (Alan Thornton); Wayland Picture Library 4, 7, 19.

Cover: foreground picture shows testing diphtheria vaccine; background picture shows HIV viruses (both photos from Science Photo Library).

CONTENTS TISSI9

A SCIENTIFIC REVOLUTION

Bright Future, or Deadly Threat?

Over the past fifty years scientists have delved into the microscopic building blocks of life, and learned how to alter the genetic structure of plants and animals. This is known as genetic engineering, and its discoveries may well be the most significant in human history.

The most enthusiastic supporters of genetic engineering say that it will rid the world of the natural ills people have suffered since they first walked the Earth. They say disease, starvation, even death itself, could be vanquished by this wonderful new science. But opponents put forward objections that are just as profound. They fear genetic engineering might unleash an ecological disaster on the world that could be even greater than nuclear war. Both sides of the argument are represented by extremely well-informed, logical individuals. So who is right, and why are there such fantastic claims for and against the science of genetic engineering?

These children may grow up to live in a world where genetic engineering is just as important as microchips and cars are today.

What are genes?

Every living thing on our planet, from blue whale to dandelion, starts life as a single fertilized cell. This cell duplicates itself to build the organism it eventually becomes.

Within the nucleus of that cell is a complex coil of material called DNA (deoxyribonucleic acid). DNA is arranged in a double-spiral sequence of units called genes, which are in turn part of a rod-shaped structure called a chromosome. In every human cell there are between 80,000 and 100,000 genes held within 46 chromosomes.

DNA is a chemical recipe for that particular organism. It tells the dandelion how to grow its stalk and fleecy top, and the whale how to grow its huge, blubbery body. In humans, too, DNA determines everything physical about us, from the colour of our hair and eyes, to our body shape and likely life expectancy.

DNA carries this recipe, or code, in a sequence of four different chemicals – identified as G, T, C and A. There are around three billion of these units, called bases, in each human cell.

Even within individual species there are slight differences in the sequence and arrangement of these chemicals, so each living thing is slightly different from any other living thing. As life reproduces, genetic codes change too. This explains why every human being alive now, and that has ever lived, is unique. (Identical twins have identical DNA, but even they have slight differences.)

This computer-generated image shows the double spiral of DNA.

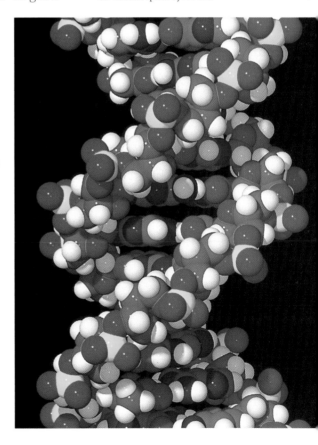

What is genetic engineering?

Today, scientists can both duplicate and change the DNA sequence within particular genes. The possibilities this has created are mind-boggling. Plants such as tomatoes can be engineered to withstand frost damage. Sheep can be engineered to produce milk that contains a valuable medicine. Humans can, in theory, be engineered so they do not pass on crippling inherited diseases to their children.

The speed with which this technology has developed has been breathtaking. People have long known that particular characteristics are passed on from one generation to another – everyone can see how children bear some resemblance to one or both of their parents. And farmers have used selective breeding to improve their produce since the days of the Ancient Egyptians. (Then, as now, farmers mated the strongest bull with other cows, for example, to produce sturdier animals.) What people didn't understand until very recently was why this happened.

Looks are only one of the characteristics we inherit from our parents. Our health, personality and intelligence are also influenced by our mother and father.

Mendel to Dolly

In the nineteenth century, the procedures of inheritance and evolution were convincingly explained by the biological research of Gregor Mendel and Charles Darwin. In the early twentieth century, scientists began to realize that chromosomes and genes were the structures which passed on characteristics from one generation to another. By the 1940s it was understood that DNA was the actual carrier of this information. A major breakthrough came in 1953 when James Watson and Francis Crick discovered the spiral helix shape of DNA itself. Once scientists knew the basic structure of what they were dealing with, they had the potential to manipulate it more effectively.

The great Victorian scientist, Charles Darwin. Along with Gregor Mendel, he laid the foundations for the science of genetics, evolution and inheritance.

Within the last half-century scientists have been able to identify specific genes, such as those causing inherited illnesses. They have gone on to clone an identical sheep (called Dolly) from a single udder cell of an adult sheep. Most extraordinary of all, they have embarked on a project to discover every single one of a human cell's 80-100,000 genes, and the three billion base units that go to make them up.

This enterprise is called the Human Genome Project, and it began in October 1990. Scientists from around the globe are participating in the programme which is expected to bring great benefits to science, industry and medicine. These include being able to identify and treat diseases much more effectively, and identify individuals more accurately from DNA samples. How this will affect us all is discussed in more detail in the chapters that follow.

FACT

There are approximately 100 million cells in every human body. Each of these cells has a nucleus that contains our entire three-billion-unit DNA code.

Mixed blessings

Throughout history, science, and its practical partner technology, have changed the way we live our lives. But scientific advances often bring mixed blessings. Primitive weapons enabled early humans to hunt creatures far more powerful than themselves. But such weapons also enabled humans to kill each other far more effectively. Sailing ships and firearms allowed European nations to cross huge oceans and discover new lands and materials, but whole cultures were destroyed or enslaved in the process. More recently, the discovery of nuclear power has provided an alternative fuel source to dwindling fossil fuel resources, but it has also provided humanity with the ability to annihilate itself and all life on Earth.

Science can be a double-edged sword. Atomic power is a useful energy source, but it can also cause unprecedented destruction.

What are ethics, and how do they affect science?

Ethics are the rules by which we live our lives. They are the standards by which human actions can be judged to be right or wrong. No civilized person would agree that it was right to kill a man to steal his wallet. But two equally intelligent and well-informed people might disagree very strongly about whether it was right to allow a doctor to inject a lethal dose of painkiller into a cancer-wracked patient who was suffering terribly and had expressed a clear wish to die.

Scientific ethics can present difficult dilemmas. During the Second World War, Nazi scientists carried out inhuman experiments on concentration camp inmates. One series of tests at Dachau, for example, studied the length of time humans could survive in freezing cold water. With brutal simplicity, the scientists left their subjects in the water until they died, and recorded how long they had managed to endure the cold.

Information from experiments such as this would be useful to scientists studying how to help airmen or sailors who had fallen or crashed into freezing water. But many people felt that it should never be used.

Others disagreed, however, and several scientists have subsequently used this Nazi data in their own research and experiments. One researcher, Dr John Hayward, Biology Professor at Victoria University in Vancouver, Canada, justified his use of the material thus: 'I don't want to have to use the Nazi data, but there is no other and will be no other in an ethical world… not to use it would be bad. I'm trying to make something constructive out of it.'

VIEWPOINTS

'… Heedless of the dangers, we are rushing full speed ahead on almost all fronts…. What has gone largely unnoticed is the unprecedented lethal threat of genetic engineering to life on the planet.'
Dr Ron Epstein. Philosophy Department. San Francisco State University. USA.

'… [There will be] fantastic benefits for humankind, some of which we can anticipate and others that will surprise us. Information generated and technologies developed will revolutionize future biological explorations.'
From the website for the Human Genome Project. United States Government Department of Energy.

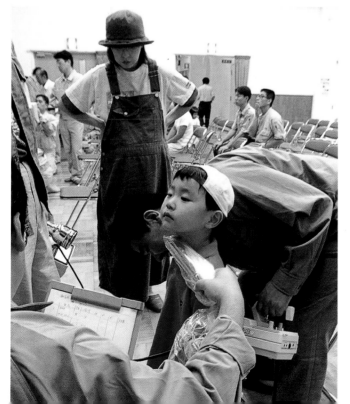

This child is being tested for radioactive exposure, following a radiation leak from a nearby nuclear power plant at Tokaimura in Japan.

Complex problems

Genetic science is also a minefield of complex ethical problems. There are fears that the possibilities it brings are too far-reaching for society to come to terms with. Should we allow people to clone themselves? Should we allow pigs with human hearts to be grown for organ transplant patients? Should we allow farmers to grow potatoes with insect genes in them, so that their goods look more appealing on the supermarket shelf?

There are huge profits to be made from genetic engineering. One projected figure estimates at least $45 billion over the next ten years. Many of the principal researchers in genetic engineering are private companies, whose major aim is to make profit. Even public universities engaged in genetic engineering research are often funded by private industry. There is the fear that the search for profits in this new technology will cause the potential hazards of genetic engineering to be overlooked. Nowhere is this more strongly felt than in the field of genetically modified food.

Genetic engineering research is both complex and costly.

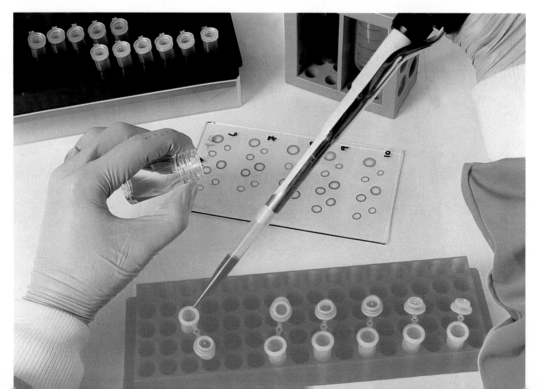

GENETICALLY MODIFIED FOOD

Food for All, or Eco-disaster?

Imagine sitting down to eat this meal…

Tomato juice with flounder gene
Catfish with trout gene, and a side order of
potatoes with waxmoth gene
Rice pudding with pea gene

As yet, none of these foods can be bought in the shops; but they have been developed in research laboratories. Perhaps, sometime in the future, they may find their way on to a supermarket shelf. Genetically modified food (sometimes known as GM food) looks and tastes exactly the same as ordinary food. Here is why the foods above would be altered in the way described.

Tomato juice with flounder gene: Flounder fish live in very cold water. Their blood contains a kind of antifreeze. Flounder genes added to tomatoes would make them more able to withstand frost.

Catfish with trout gene: Trout genes enable catfish to grow faster. Catfish farmers could produce and sell them much quicker.

Potatoes with waxmoth gene: Potatoes bruise easily when they are being transported. The waxmoth gene would reduce bruising.

Rice pudding with pea gene: Pea gene added to rice would increase its nutritional content.

Genetic engineering in plants and animals is possible because all genes, no matter where they come from, are made of the same basic material – DNA. The DNA from two different organisms can be spliced together. Here is a simplified explanation of how flounder genes could be added to tomatoes to make them frost resistant.

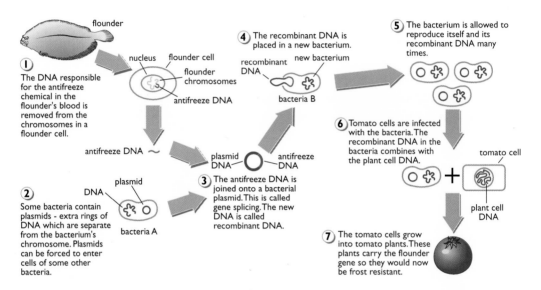

flounder

1 The DNA responsible for the antifreeze chemical in the flounder's blood is removed from the chromosomes in a flounder cell.

nucleus flounder cell

flounder chromosomes

antifreeze DNA

4 The recombinant DNA is placed in a new bacterium.

recombinant DNA

new bacterium

bacteria B

5 The bacterium is allowed to reproduce itself and its recombinant DNA many times.

antifreeze DNA ~

2 Some bacteria contain plasmids - extra rings of DNA which are separate from the bacterium's chromosome. Plasmids can be forced to enter cells of some other bacteria.

DNA

plasmid

bacteria A

plasmid DNA antifreeze DNA

3 The antifreeze DNA is joined onto a bacterial plasmid. This is called gene splicing. The new DNA is called recombinant DNA.

6 Tomato cells are infected with the bacteria. The recombinant DNA in the bacteria combines with the plant cell DNA.

tomato cell

plant cell DNA

7 The tomato cells grow into tomato plants. These plants carry the flounder gene so they would now be frost resistant.

Back to reality

This may be the future, but what about now? The agriculture industry, especially in the United States and China, has shown a great deal of interest in making use of genetic technology. Genetically modified soya, tomato and maize crops have been grown, and cheese has also been produced using GM ingredients. Recent research suggests that, worldwide, at least 28 million hectares of agricultural land have been turned over to GM crop production.

At the moment, the main reasons for giving plants and animals new genes are to encourage speedy growth, make them more nutritious, cut down on damage from insects and weeds, and reduce the need for herbicide and pesticide usage. Genetic engineering in agriculture means more food, quicker, and at lower cost to the farmer and (hopefully) the consumer.

Billion dollar industry

Several huge agricultural companies have invested millions of dollars in producing genetically engineered products. One of the best known is an American company called Monsanto. Their company slogan is 'Food Health Hope'. Here are some of their recent products.

- Cotton protected from insect infestation with Bollgard® gene, which keeps the plant free of cotton bollworm.
- Newleaf® potatoes which are poisonous to Colorado potato beetles.
- Soybeans, cotton and corn with Roundup Ready® gene to tolerate Roundup® herbicide. This means that a farmer can use the powerful Roundup® herbicide, which will kill all other plants (weeds) but leave his Roundup Ready® plants unharmed.

VIEWPOINTS

'[Genetic engineering is taking mankind] into realms that belong to God and God alone. If something goes badly wrong, we will be faced with the problem of clearing up a kind of pollution which is self-perpetuating. I am not convinced that anyone has the first idea of how this could be done, or indeed who would have to pay.'
HRH Prince Charles on genetically modified food.

'Novartis only applies procedures involving gene technology when they bring a clear superiority over conventional products for the benefit of patients, customers, consumers, as well as society as a whole.'
Novartis Seeds AG, in their promotional brochure: Maize is Maize. Why we use gene technology.

Testing genetically modified maize. This batch has been engineered to be resistant to a herbicide that kills all the surrounding weeds.

This Filipino farmer is battling desperately to stop a swarm of locusts from destroying his rice crop.

Farmers wage an endless war against choking weeds and ravenous insects. In many parts of the world twenty per cent or more of every crop is lost before it is harvested. In some years, pests can destroy entire harvests. Genetically modified products offer farmers the opportunity to grow, and hence sell, more of their produce. Genetically modified plants are engineered to need fewer pesticides and herbicides. This should mean that farmers would need to spray their crops far less than before. Crop sprays are expensive. Overall, the use of GM plants should be cheaper for the farmer and mean less pollution to the environment.

The ability to grow more food is particularly important in view of the world's growing population. At the moment the number of people in the world increases by ninety million every year. It has already reached six billion.

So what's the problem?
Manufacturers of GM foods claim that their products are environmentally friendly and the food produced by genetic engineering is safe to eat. Yet

no area of biotechnology is causing more concern. Why are people so worried about genetic engineering and agriculture?

Genetic engineering is 'shuffling the deck of genes' in ways that are entirely new, and creating living things that have never existed before. The problems this may cause are difficult to predict. Many new technologies come with this risk. For example, when pesticides were first produced in the 1950s, they were hailed as a miracle cure for pest problems. But as time went by, it was discovered that some pesticides could also cause birds to lay deformed eggs and humans to develop cancer. The insects they were supposed to kill also developed a resistance to pesticides.

Genetically engineered crops can sometimes pollinate other non-engineered crops nearby. It is feared that this will influence the evolution of local pests and wildlife. For example, if other local

VIEWPOINTS

'It [the GM food industry] is bad science working together with big business for quick profit....'
Dr Mae-Wan Ho. Head of the Bio-Electrodynamics Laboratory. Open University. UK.

'The simple arithmetic is that we're going to double the population, and we're not going to increase the amount of land under cultivation. You have to get two times as much production from every acre of land that you get today....'
Robert Shapiro. Chief Executive Officer at Monsanto.

Concern over GM foods is worldwide. This Greenpeace protestor is holding stalks of genetically modified maize during a protest in France.

plants inherit herbicide resistance from a crop genetically engineered to have this characteristic, it will be much more difficult to remove them. In the past, weeds and pests built up a resistance to herbicides and pesticides. Environmental campaigners fear that cross-pollination may create super weeds and super pests that may be extremely difficult to remove or destroy.

Unnatural foods?

Some supporters of the genetic modification of plants and animals claim that this technology is no different from the selective breeding and cross-breeding that farmers have practised since ancient times. Opponents say this is misleading: traditional methods of cross-breeding depend on natural species compatibility. Genetically engineered plants and animals often contain gene combinations that would never naturally occur. These new foods have never been part of the human food supply, and the long-term effects of such genetic mutations are completely unknown.

Opponents of GM food say that these mutations can produce harmful toxins, and unforeseen and unknown allergens. They point to one of the very first GM foods to be sold commercially – a dietary supplement called tryptophan. This was made by a Japanese company in the late 1980s, using genetically engineered bacteria. Thousands of people who took tryptophan began to suffer from neurological problems. At least 1,500 were permanently disabled and 37 died. There is some controversy over whether this was caused by genetic modification or part of the manufacturing process. Whatever the cause, the incident harmed the image of GM food.

One product recently researched by biotechnology companies was the so-called 'terminator seed', to be used in grain crops such as corn or wheat. These seeds grow once, but do not produce plants whose seeds can be replanted. This means that a farmer must buy new seeds every time he wants to grow that particular crop.

At the moment, all farmers replant seeds from previous crops – this has been part of agricultural practice since farming began. In some parts of the world, such as India, as much as eighty per cent of the grain harvest is kept for replanting. The idea of 'terminator seeds' has caused a great deal of concern and anger, particularly in poorer countries.

In research laboratories some animals have been genetically engineered to be much larger than they would be naturally. This means that fish farmers, for example, could produce salmon that are larger than wild salmon. Environmentalists fear that, if such fish escaped into the wild, they would soon replace the smaller local salmon and would eat far more of the available food. This could upset the balance of the environment in ways that are hard to predict.

VIEWPOINTS

'The safety studies that are required for the approval of genetically altered plants are a guarantee that the food products that are produced from them will be as healthy and safe as conventional products.'
Susanne Lauber Fürst. Federation of the Swiss Food Industry.

'THEY get giant profits. All WE get is a new and uncertain environment – an end to the world as we know it.'
The environmental group Greenpeace.

GM *food could prove to be extremely useful to peoples of the world threatened by starvation.*

DEBATE

Would a vegetable containing animal genes still be a vegetable? If you were a vegetarian, would you be prepared to eat foods containing animal genes?

Public suspicion

The controversy over GM foods is causing problems for the manufacturers of these products. Even supporters of GM food are concerned by some of the issues raised, and the negative public perception of these products. Professor Gordon Conway, President of the Rockefeller Foundation, a charitable organization dedicated to helping poor countries, sees GM foods as an essential weapon against hunger. He feels that many of the dangers are exaggerated. But he still had this to say in a speech to Monsanto's board of directors in 1999: '[Use of GM foods] is being threatened by the mounting controversies in Europe and… the United States. Underlying… this… are genuine concerns about the ethical consequences of biotechnology, and fears for the environment and about the potential impact on human health. …Only if you are seen to be careful, concerned, interested and open-minded will you convince the reasonable majority that you are partners to be trusted in looking for new ways to feed people without creating health problems that are worse than hunger.'

These genetically altered strawberry seedlings are being engineered to have a greater resistance to pesticides.

Monsanto were prepared to listen. In October 1999 they announced that they would not be developing or selling their version of the 'terminator seed'. At the time of writing, the whole GM food business seems under threat. Bowing to consumer pressure, many UK supermarkets have withdrawn food products containing GM ingredients, and in the United States many people are feeling increasingly uneasy about GM foods. It could be that a beneficial and potentially extremely useful technology has been nipped in the bud by a simple fear of the unknown. Only time, and further research, will tell whether people's fears are based on reality.

VIEWPOINTS

'You can stop splitting the atom; you can stop visiting the moon; you can stop using aerosols. But you cannot recall a new form of life.'
Edwin Chargoff, geneticist.

'Agriculture is the only hope for India.... In the next century, we must produce more from less land. If nothing is done, India will move into chaos.'
Professor Swaminathan, Centre for Research on Sustainable Agriculture, Madras, talking in favour of GM food.

Consumer resistance to GM foods has been so great that many major supermarkets have withdrawn them from sale.

GENETICS
AND COMMERCE

Good Business, or Bio-Piracy?

Steam power shaped the nineteenth century. It drove the machines that brought about the Industrial Revolution, and propelled the steam trains and boats that made travel quicker and cheaper than ever before. In the twentieth century, electricity transformed people's lives. It powered everything from street lights to washing machines, and enabled scientists to invent the television and computer. Genetic engineering is expected to have a similarly massive influence on the history of the twenty-first century.

New products
Vast amounts of money are spent on developing and purchasing biotechnology products for agriculture. Medicine is the other major area of research (featured in later chapters of this book). But elsewhere, other so-called 'life-science' companies have been creating yet more extraordinary products. For example:

- genetically modified bacteria to clean up oil spilled into the environment; the bacteria break down complex oil molecules into more harmless and easily dispersed substances;
- an enzyme (a protein produced by a living cell) engineered to eat chemical waste;
- an enzyme to extract minerals such as gold and copper from raw materials;
- a bacterium which could transform waste products into ethanol fuel.

Saving energy

The new science promises to have endlessly useful applications. For instance, many industrial processes involve taking raw materials and turning them into usable products. This can often be a complex and expensive process. When paper is made, for example, wood pulp needs to be treated with chemicals to break it down. The process creates a great deal of chemical waste, which then has to be treated before it can be disposed of. One possible use of genetic engineering would be to engineer trees that produce wood pulp which is easier to break down. This means that fewer chemicals and less time and effort would be expended on the pulping process.

Another potential use of this new science would be the manufacture of materials that are currently made from oil, such as plastic. Like coal and gas, oil is a fossil fuel, and supplies are expected to run out soon. Scientists are currently investigating the production of plastic via living organisms such as bacteria, and even potatoes.

A technician operates a test fermentation unit in a biotechnology laboratory. Once perfected, such equipment may make genetically engineered products in industrial scale quantities.

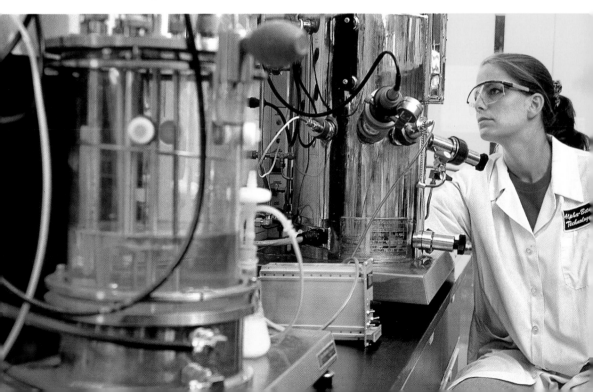

Bioprospecting

Whenever a new science has a major impact on people's lives, there is money to be made. Genetic engineering is expected to generate many billions of dollars. All of the developments mentioned earlier are undoubtedly useful and promising, but there are aspects of biotechnology and business which are causing a great deal of concern.

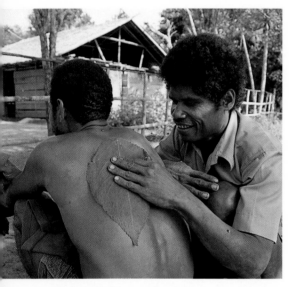

In Indonesia, this particular plant offers relief from rheumatism.

Many biotechnology companies are currently trawling through the wildlife of Africa and South America, searching for plants and animals with genetic traits that they can develop into saleable products. This is known as 'bioprospecting'. They hope that somewhere in the remote rainforests and mountains of the southern hemisphere there may be a cure for diseases such as AIDS and cancers. They are also sampling the blood, hair and saliva of people in remote forest and hill tribes in case any useful genetic material can be gained this way.

Genetic engineering gives science and industry the chance to transform inexpensive raw materials into highly desirable products. But critics of bioprospecting see this as yet another way in which wealthy, western nations are exploiting poorer developing countries. They describe such research as 'biopiracy'.

This kind of exploitation is not just confined to developing countries. In 1990 an American named John Moore was dying of a rare disease called hairy cell leukaemia. His spleen had swollen to forty times its normal weight, and his doctors expected him to die. Moore recovered. This was because his blood produced unusually high quantities of healing proteins, such as interferon and interleukin, which stimulate the body's immune system. This gave him the ability to survive an illness that would have killed almost anybody else. Interferon and interleukin are given to cancer and AIDS patients and are extremely expensive to manufacture. John Moore was a natural goldmine.

Without his consent, Moore's doctor isolated and patented these rare genetic properties in his blood, and then sold them to a pharmaceutical company for $15 million. This company has gone on to make more than $3 billion from medicine derived from Moore's blood.

When Moore found out, he took his doctor to court. The case went as far as the California Supreme Court and they ruled that the medicine produced from Moore's blood was his doctor's invention, and not Moore's property. He received no compensation at all.

Copyright on life

The bioprospectors at work in the rainforests and the medical researchers in western hospitals and universities are all racing to discover useful genetic traits that they can claim as their own invention. They do this by taking out a patent on this knowledge. (A patent is a government document granting the right to a company to be the sole user and seller of a particular invention for a limited period.)

The first patent for a genetically engineered organism was issued in 1971 by the United States government for a bacterium for cleaning up oil spills. Since then, patents have been given on hundreds of genetically engineered plants and animals and, as in the case of John Moore, on human genes.

FACT

Bill Gates, the world's richest man, has invested heavily in genetic engineering projects. He compares mapping the human genome to deciphering an extremely complex computer programme.

In Guinea, West Africa, the bark from this tree is used to make local medicines. Biotechnology companies are looking in the developing world for plants with genetic traits that they can develop into saleable products.

Discovery or invention?

What people disagree about is whether genes are discoveries or inventions. Some people feel that identifying something that is there already is a discovery, rather than an invention. Genetic engineering companies say that research is extremely expensive; they argue that they should be assured some return on the time and money they have spent unearthing a useful gene and working out how to make practical use of it.

To some observers, this seems illogical. Jeremy Rifkin of the Foundation on Economic Trends, a Washington pressure group which has strongly criticized the patenting of genetic information, had this to say: 'No reasonable person would dare suggest that a scientist who isolated, classified and described the properties of hydrogen, helium or oxygen should be granted exclusive right, for twenty years, to claim the substance as a human invention. [Yet the US Patent Office] has… said that the isolation and classification of a gene's properties and purposes is sufficient to claim it as an invention.'

Multinational business

Many of the companies researching and producing genetic engineering products are multinational businesses. Many multinationals are actually wealthier than a lot of countries. (In 1999, for example, fifty-one of the world's hundred largest economies were multinational companies, rather than countries.) Such immense wealth brings so much power and influence that some governments, particularly in the developing world, are reluctant to challenge multinational companies, even if they believe that what they are doing is wrong. Critics feel that this inability to challenge the power of the multinationals hampers criticism of genetic engineering right across the spectrum – from food production to medical research and cloning.

Compromising independence

Another complication is that much research into genetic engineering is carried out in universities, which are set up as public assets to create and share their knowledge for the benefit of all society. However, a lot of this research is paid for by private companies, who exist to make a profit. Many people feel that the public universities are compromising their independence by allowing their research to be funded in this way.

One major concern is that potential risks in genetic engineering will be overlooked by academics who are anxious to maintain their funding, or who fear that speaking out against the work their department is doing will damage their careers.

Protestors at the World Trade Organization conference in Seattle, 1999. Many people fear that multinational corporations will misuse genetic engineering products.

GENETICS AND WARFARE

Necessary Evil, or Crime Against Nature?

The use of chemical and biological weapons in warfare has always caused particular revulsion. Their grisly and indiscriminate nature, and potential for long-term or irreparable damage, makes them especially sinister and morally unsettling.

In medieval times, wells were polluted, and plague-ridden corpses were catapulted into besieged cities to spread infection. In the twentieth century, poisonous gas was used against soldiers and civilians, and chemical defoliants (which destroy vegetation) were sprayed over territory to deprive the enemy of both cover and food supplies. At the turn of the millennium, biotechnology is helping to create genetically engineered bacteria and viruses which could prove to be the deadliest biological weapons yet. Currently, research is being conducted into the use of such infectious organisms as HIV (the virus that causes AIDS), hantaviruses such as Ebola (which causes fatal internal bleeding), and the 'flesh-eating' streptococcus bacterium.

New weapons

Genetic engineering could develop pathogens (disease-carrying organisms) that have greater resistance to antibiotics, can survive for longer in more hostile conditions than they would naturally, and are more difficult to identify. Most

US warplanes spraying defoliants during the Vietnam War. Such biological weapons still cause damage decades after they are deployed.

alarmingly, pathogens such as HIV, or the flesh-eating streptococcus, which are currently transmitted via body fluids, could be engineered to cause infection via the air, in a similar way to a cold or flu. This is the most effective way of delivering biological weapons, and would make them particularly lethal when used against a city.

The thought of large civilian populations being deliberately exposed to flesh-eating bacteria is terrifying. But so far, such technology has yet to be developed. There is still a great gap between understanding an organism, and being able to control it. However, advances in genetic engineering are occurring at breathtaking speed, and each breakthrough makes such nightmare scenarios seem all too possible.

Some scientists fear that genetically engineered bioweapons have already been used. They think there is evidence to suggest that Iraq deployed them against Allied troops during the Gulf War of 1991, and that they are the cause of so-called 'Gulf War Syndrome' (a mystery illness that has affected thousands of Allied soldiers in the years following the conflict).

VIEWPOINTS

'Any discovery in pathology... can be applied to benefit mankind or misapplied for a malevolent purpose.'
Mark Wheelis, bioweapons historian, University of California, USA.

'Scientific researchers have a responsibility for the use to which their discoveries are put.'
Dr Ron Epstein, Philosophy Department, San Francisco State University, USA.

Iraqi Kurds fall victim to nerve gas attack. Ruthless regimes may soon have far worse weapons at their disposal, thanks to genetic engineering.

Dr Garth Nicolson, Professor of Pathology at the M D Anderson Cancer Clinic in Houston, Texas, suggests that the syndrome has been produced by a variation of the HIV virus. He also speculates that such a pathogen was actually manufactured in the United States, and sold to Iraq in the 1980s. (During this time Iraq was fighting Iran, one of the United States' most fervent opponents, and the US gave military aid to Iraq.)

Soldiers during the Gulf War, wearing clothing designed to protect them from biological and chemical weapons.

FACT

Around 70,000 Gulf War veterans claim to be suffering from Gulf War Syndrome. Most experts believe the illness has been caused by exposure to chemicals from burning oil wells, or poisons linked to inoculations given as a counter measure against possible bioweapon use.

In South Africa before the end of the apartheid regime in the late twentieth century, the government ordered research into a biological weapon that would kill only black people. Although such a weapon was never developed, genetic engineering makes such a monstrosity conceivable. It is theoretically possible to doctor a virus that would only activate itself in a host body with specific genetic racial traits, such as hair colour, skin colour, or whatever.

Further research?
Many people would argue that to carry out research into such a dreadful use of technology was morally wrong. But is there a choice? Many commentators on genetic engineering see the science as a genie which has escaped from its bottle and cannot be returned. Once the technology has been developed, genetically engineered biological weapons are relatively easy to manufacture. Almost any country, and even terrorist groups, could make and use them. There is a fine line between developing defensive

biowarfare protection (which is what the United States claims it is doing) and making offensive biowarfare weapons. It is also fairly easy to turn biotechnology laboratories and pharmaceutical factories from producers of medical supplies in peacetime into manufacturers of deadly pathogens for use in biowarfare.

In the United States, the government justifies research into genetically engineered weapons with its declared intention to maintain a technological advantage, and hence military superiority, over any likely enemy. The logic is that if American scientists do not carry out research into such bioweapons, they will not be able to provide a means of defence against them.

Biological exodus
The threat that bioweapons could be used in modern warfare might be all too real. During the Cold War (a period from 1945-89 during which the United States and the Soviet Union were extremely distrustful of one another) both the United States and the Soviet Union developed deadly biological weapons. When the Soviet Union collapsed in 1989, there were over 30,000 Soviet scientists working on biological weapon production. In the economic chaos that followed, many were tempted to take their knowledge and experience abroad. Some were lured away to work on biological weapons research in countries such as China, Iraq and Iran.

Since the first atomic weapons were used against Japan at the end of the Second World War in 1945, the spectre of nuclear annihilation has hung over the world. Fear of nuclear weapons comes and goes as international tensions ebb and flow. Perhaps the twenty-first century will be haunted by the even more deadly threat of genetically engineered bioweapons?

VIEWPOINTS

'After they became aware of the horrors of nuclear war, many of the scientists who... developed the first atomic bomb underwent terrible anguish and soul-searching. It is surprising that more geneticists do not see the parallels.'
Dr Ron Epstein, Philosophy Department, San Francisco State University, USA.

'I don't see how we'd be talking about the ethics of genetic engineering, any more than that of iron smelting – which can be used to build bridges or guns.'
Dr Joshua Lederberg, Nobel laureate in genetics, Rockefeller University, USA.

DEBATE

Is the idea of a race-germ any worse than the neutron bomb of the 1980s – which was developed to kill people but leave buildings intact?

GENETICS AND CIVIL LIBERTIES

DNA Testing - Good or Bad?

Who's keeping tabs on you? The government records your birth, marriage and death. Your school or college keeps information about your attendance and academic achievements. Your doctor has a file detailing your state of health, which he or she glances over each time you visit. If you own a car, information about it is kept on computer. A police officer on the street can call from a radio and check ownership of any suspicious looking vehicle within minutes. The police also keep fingerprint records. In the future, government authorities or companies could also be checking your genetic makeup.

Ten years from now, everyone's genetic information could be stored in one huge national database. Such a record would be invaluable to medical researchers, whose work would benefit immeasurably from such a bonanza of raw material. The police, too, would be able to use this information to identify criminals. For example, everyone sheds hair and skin cells wherever they go. Despite their best efforts, burglars would be likely to leave evidence of their presence in a house, giving police a 'genetic fingerprint' which a powerful computer could easily identify. Unless you are an identical twin your DNA is unique, so such evidence would assist the police immeasurably in apprehending criminals.

There could be other uses too. A company hiring staff could examine their candidates' genes. They could check who was likely to do well at the job and who was likely to steal from the cash till. An insurance company could decide whether a new client was a good or bad risk. They could check whether the prospective client was likely to live to 95, or drop dead at 40. But is this likely to happen?

It's happened already. In the United States, people have been denied health insurance and employment because they have 'bad genes'. The armed services also take DNA tests of every new recruit. 'Fear of discrimination is real but exaggerated,' says David Christianson of the American Academy of Actuaries. (Actuaries assess risks for insurance companies.) He says genetic testing can actually help people too. For example, someone with a family history of a crippling disease might be refused health insurance, on the grounds that statistically they would be likely to develop that illness. Genetic testing might indicate that the disease had not been passed on to them, and they would then be able to obtain insurance cover.

Cold facts

Nationwide databases are also becoming a reality. In Iceland the government has authorized a huge information gathering project by the Icelandic genetic engineering company, deCode Genetics.

Viewing DNA on a computer monitor. It has been treated to appear as different-shaded strips.

These researchers are using microscopes and video monitors to analyze DNA taken from people with inherited diseases.

They are currently attempting to collect the genetic code of every person in the country. This material comes in the form of blood samples from volunteers, and other sources such as medical records. This huge database provides invaluable information for researchers looking for the genetic causes of illnesses such as diabetes, osteoporosis and even schizophrenia.

But not everyone is happy; in fact one third of the country's doctors have refused to co-operate with the company. Many academics, too, feel the project is wrong. Einar Arnason, Professor of Population Genetics at the University of Iceland, recently commented: 'It is in the commercial interest of a company to sell (genetic) information to the highest bidder, presumably – and that is not necessarily in the public interest'.

The UK government also has plans for a centralized national collection of DNA. Samples could be gathered from genetic databases already in existence (for example, there are 40,000 people on a cystic fibrosis DNA database), and blood donors and doctor's patients would also be asked if they would like to contribute. The intention would be eventually to include everyone in the country.

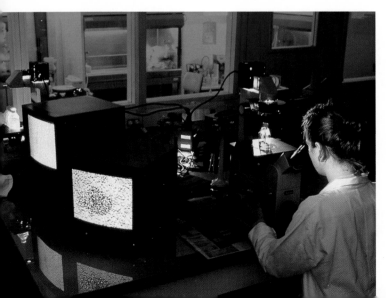

Discussing the proposed DNA collection on British television's *Newsnight*, Dr Karl Stefansson of deCode Genetics commented: 'It is the kind of information the medical research community has used to create new knowledge for a century, and without which we would not have medicine as we know it today.' But he also admitted, despite claims to confidentiality, that: 'You can never guarantee that someone's genetic map will remain anonymous forever.'

Recently, other research into confidential and highly personal medical matters has shown how difficult it is to keep such information secret. HIV screening of pregnant women in the UK was supposedly anonymous, but it proved possible to trace those taking part.

Bad risks

Currently it is not permissible for UK employers or insurance companies to gain access to a client or candidate's medical or genetic record. However, as testing techniques become easier and cheaper, it is quite possible to imagine companies insisting on a person having such a test before a policy or job was offered. Dr Richard Nicholson, editor of the *Bulletin of Medical Ethics*, believes a national database will discriminate against those with potentially serious genetic disorders. He fears insurance companies, in particular, will go to great lengths to discover their clients' genetic history. 'It is inevitable, because insurance companies are going to want to gather every little bit of information about someone they are going to insure'.

DEBATE

Should employers be allowed to check the genetic records of their staff? Should an airline, for example, be allowed to check a pilot for any predisposition to heart attack or stroke? After all, if a pilot dies during a landing or takeoff, then the plane and all the passengers are in grave danger.

This equipment is being used in gene therapy research for cystic fibrosis.

The rights and wrongs of such procedures are further complicated by the fact that genetic tests can only indicate a likelihood of a particular illness or personal characteristic. People may well be discriminated against for traits they are never actually going to develop.

GENETICS AND MEDICINE

Medical miracle, or waste of money?

Sheep producing medicine in their milk; bacteria making insulin for diabetics; a gene to make a damaged heart repair itself; medicine is beginning to use all of these extraordinary genetic engineering techniques, and there are more to come. Transplant patients could have tailor-made organs grown for them in animals. Babies with terrible inherited diseases could be cured while still in the womb. Even the inevitable process of ageing could be halted.

These genetically engineered plants produce proteins to protect humans from specific viruses.

Aside from the way in which we produce food, no other area of our lives will be more affected by genetic engineering than health care. It promises nothing less than a new era in medicine. Instead of treating the symptoms of an illness, that illness could be treated at its most fundamental level – in the genetic make-up of the patient. Genetic engineering could cure us of some diseases before we even become ill.

What's going on?
Much of this new medicine will result from research currently being done on the Human Genome Project. Many independent universities and medical research companies are also engaged in cutting-edge genetic exploration. Here are some of the more recent developments:

- **Drug production**. Many drugs are now manufactured using genetic engineering techniques. There are two main methods:

Gene cloning (also known as recombinant DNA technique). Useful DNA is inserted into the DNA of fast-breeding bacteria. These bacteria then produce medically beneficial proteins. Insulin, which is an essential drug for diabetics, is mainly manufactured in this way.

Pharming. This means using animals or plants to make medicine. (The word is a combination of 'pharmaceutics', meaning the preparation of drugs, and 'farming'.) For example, a sheep has been genetically engineered to produce a drug called alpha-1-antitripsin. This is a protein used for the treatment of cystic fibrosis – a disease that causes the lungs to become clogged with mucus. Maize and tobacco plants are currently being developed to produce human antibodies – defensive chemicals that help the body fight infection.

- **Cancer treatment**. One treatment for cancer, called chemotherapy, requires a patient to take a drug that kills cancer cells. The drug often damages healthy cells too, and can be very unpleasant for the patient. A gene could be introduced into the body to protect healthy cells from the chemotherapy, but leave cancer cells unprotected. Scientists have also recently discovered one gene which protects the body against cancerous chemicals. This could lead to the development of a cancer prevention pill.

These fermentation vats manufacture genetically engineered hepatitis vaccine.

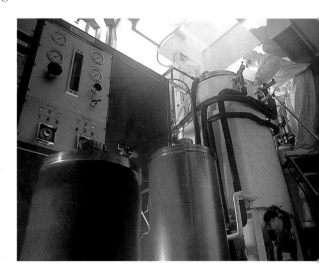

- **Vaccine production**. Most medicines are given to relieve symptoms of an illness, whereas vaccines prevent an illness developing in the first place. The process involves giving the patient a small dose of a disease, and allowing the body to develop an immunity to it. Making a vaccine can be time-consuming and expensive, but genetic engineering will enable pharmaceutical companies to make vaccines more quickly and cheaply.

- **Genetic screening**. Screening means looking for illnesses before they develop. Huge advances are expected here, thanks to the work of the Human Genome Project.

- **Skin grafts**. Genetically engineered human skin is being produced commercially by Novartis – a biotechnology company best known for its production of GM crops. The product is called Apligraf®. It is grown from donor cells of healthy skin, and used in skin grafts.

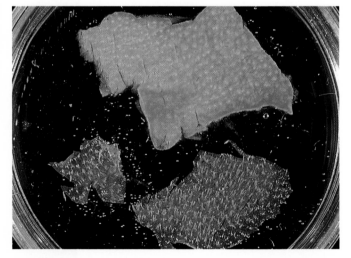

Human skin being grown in a petri dish. This synthetic skin can be used to treat burn victims.

- **Stem cell research**. When the first fetal cells in the womb begin to grow into a baby, each cell has the ability to become any kind of body organ or tissue. One cell can turn into a hair cell, heart cell, skin cell, or whatever. These cells are called stem cells, and when the fetus is fully developed they switch themselves off. Research is currently going on into how to switch these cells back on, and make them regenerate damaged tissue.

For example, when a heart grows inside an embryo, a gene tells it how to make its arteries. This gene can be reactivated in the hearts of patients with blocked arteries. The gene is tricked into behaving like it did when it was constructing the embryo heart, and it grows new blood vessels within the heart. This means that a life-threatening heart operation may be avoided. This very new technique has actually been tested in the USA.

Stem cell treatment, if it develops as planned, will have far-reaching effects on degenerative illnesses such as Parkinson's, Alzheimer's, multiple sclerosis and stroke. It can also potentially cure other afflictions of old age, such as failing hearing and eyesight, and arthritis.

- **Gene therapy**. Inherited illnesses, such as Hodgkinson's disease, Parkinson's disease and sickle cell anaemia, affect millions of people. These afflictions are caused by defective genes, which are passed on to a baby by one or both of its parents. Such diseases could be treated or even eradicated with a technique called gene therapy.

> ## FACT
> Human beings have over 80,000 genes. Yet many inherited illnesses, such as Huntington's disease, are passed from parent to child by a single faulty gene.

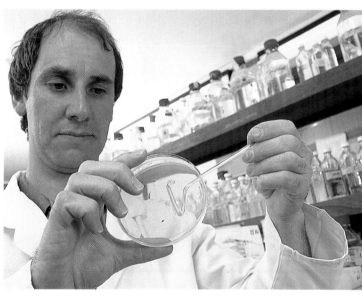

This researcher is working on developing an AIDS vaccine using genetically modified bacteria.

There are two types of gene therapy:

Somatic gene therapy. Healthy, desirable genes are introduced to replace faulty genes in specific body cells, such as those in the lungs causing cystic fibrosis. This is done via a vector – a means of delivering these genes to the faulty body cells that need them. (A vector is usually a modified virus which can no longer cause disease or replicate itself.) In somatic gene therapy for cystic fibrosis, a type of virus called an adenovirus is used, because it flourishes in the lungs. Somatic gene therapy is currently being used effectively on patients.

Germline gene therapy. Here, faulty genes in the body's 'germ cells' – sperms and eggs – are altered. This means that any changes will be passed on to the patient's children. So far, tests have proved effective on mice. Germline gene therapy has not yet been tried on humans. The possibility of producing a deformed child is still too great. The treatment also has far-reaching consequences. Many people feel it is wrong to pass on engineered changes, with possible unknown side effects, to future generations.

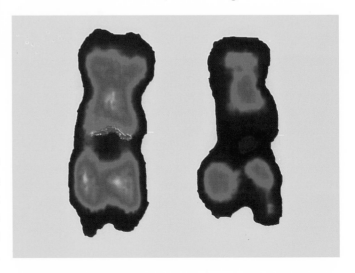

This false-colour photograph shows a healthy gene (on the left), and one linked to the development of breast cancer (on the right). Anyone inheriting the gene on the right is at higher risk of contracting this illness.

Not all good

Few people would argue that advances in the treatment of incurable diseases are a bad thing. But inevitably there are problems. Genetic engineering research is a costly, high-technology pursuit. It is possible that many of its benefits (stem cell treatment, for example) will only be available to wealthy patients in the initial stages. Many people feel that medical research should concentrate on cheap, low-technology cures, which will have immediate benefit to millions of people.

Gene therapy is an intricate, complex procedure. Here a technician uses a microscope to introduce a healthy gene into a vector.

Another aspect of medical genetic engineering that causes a great deal of concern is the possible use of animals as donors for human organ transplants. Why is this being considered? When a new organ is placed in a patient, their body's immune system rejects it. The white blood cells, which are programmed to fight all intruders into the body, recognize the cells of the new organ as foreign, so they attack it. To combat this, transplant patients are given drugs to weaken their own immune system. This makes them more prone to other illnesses, and may lead to their death.

One solution to this problem would be to grow a donor animal, such as a pig, which had some of the patient's genes in its genetic makeup. In this way, when the organ was transplanted, the body's immune system would accept it as its own. The research for this technique has not yet been permitted to reach clinical trials in the UK, although it is theoretically possible to carry it out in other countries.

Equipment such as this is used to research potential human/animal organ transplants.

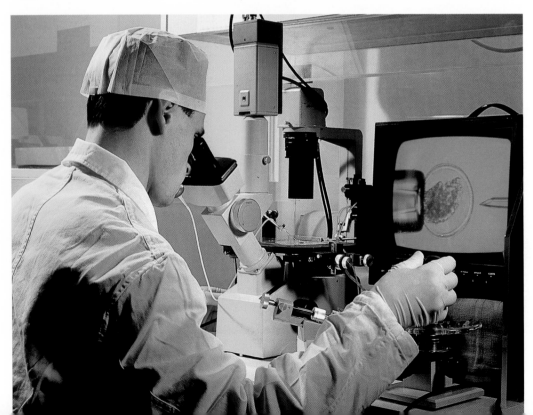

Some people are revolted by the idea of a human
being with a pig's heart. Others think it would be
wrong to create an animal for such a task. (With
millions of pigs being killed every year for food, it
is difficult to see why pig donors should be a special
case.) Questions also arise about how human an
animal with human genes actually is. Would killing
it be murder? Would eating it be cannibalism?

There are practical problems too. Other research that
has treated people with animal tissues led to patients
being infected by Creutzfeldt-Jakob disease, the same
illness that is passed on to humans by BSE-infected
beef. Some viruses only affect certain animals and do
not harm humans. But viruses are mutating all the
time, and scientists are concerned that animals with
human genes will provide an opportunity for animal
viruses to mutate into pathogens that will be capable
of attacking humans.

Human factories
Peering into the future, other issues raise further
uncomfortable questions. One pharmaceutical
company recently tried to patent the concept of a
'pharm-woman'. Just as sheep are genetically
engineered to produce beneficial drugs, so women can
be made to produce similar drugs in their own breast
milk. The idea of a person being turned into a human
drug factory is deeply disturbing to many people.

In the last century, we saw hugely powerful
totalitarian regimes behave with extraordinary
cruelty to conquered populations and their own
citizens alike. It is very easy to imagine a future
regime with a similar fanaticism having no qualms
about using such biotechnology. Regardless of
whatever regime might be in power, some people
would become human drug factories entirely
voluntarily. After all, in poorer countries people
already sell their body organs to make money.

Who wants to live forever?

Finally, advances in our understanding of the mechanism of DNA open yet another avenue – the possibility of immortality. The Geron Corporation, a vast 'life-science' company, is currently engaged in anti-ageing research. They are concentrating their work on 'telomeres' – coded sequences in chromosomes, which become shorter every time a cell divides. This causes cells to stop reproducing themselves as we grow older. Having discovered the molecular mechanism of ageing, researchers are now concentrating on stopping these telomeres from getting shorter.

The Geron Corporation has succeeded with skin cells. Because their telomeres do not get shorter, the cells should be able to carry on dividing forever. A person with such skin cells would have skin that never aged. There is more to ageing than young-looking skin, but as science advances, who knows what sort of anti-ageing techniques might be developed?

Cosmetics to fight the effects of ageing sell in huge quantities. Research into delaying or stopping the genetic causes of ageing may soon reap huge financial rewards.

A product that delayed or stopped the ageing process would undoubtedly appeal to a lot of people, and be taken up by many rich enough to afford it. But a population that lived way beyond a normal life span might be disastrous for society as a whole. People are already living longer. In the UK, for example, the over sixty-fives in the population will increase by fifty per cent over the next three decades. This will place enormous burdens on a country's pension and health care systems. Even if genetic engineering techniques mean the ageing population is healthier, and needs less money spent on medical care, who will pay the pensions of all these additional people? Living for much longer may sound like an attractive option, but it may create appalling problems for any society with a population rich enough to invest in such treatment.

Today many people are living longer, healthier lives. There may soon be genetic engineering techniques that enable us to live even longer.

DEBATE

The world's population already exceeds six billion. Should we really be looking into techniques which allow some people to lead even longer lives?

GENETIC PERFECTION

Superhuman, or super-inhuman?

VIEWPOINTS

'If we can make better human beings by knowing how to add genes, why shouldn't we do it? The biggest ethical problem we have is not using our knowledge.'
James Watson. Nobel prize-winning geneticist.

'This... induces the fear that genetic testing will create a "blue blood class", with a biological reinforcement of their class distinction.'
UC Davis website. 'The Pros and Cons of Genetic Engineering'.

Everybody, and every living thing, has a handful of defective genes in their DNA. In a sequence of three billion human bases, a few are bound to be wrong. In most cases the defect goes unnoticed, or is too minor to cause a problem, but sometimes physical changes are evident. Scientists think this is one way in which living things evolve – a genetic irregularity can actually provide a beneficial twist, which enables the carrier of that gene to survive and reproduce far more effectively. But there is a downside too. Faulty genes cause many birth defects. Down's and Williams' syndrome children owe their learning difficulties and uncommon physical appearance to changes in their DNA.

This child has Down's syndrome, a medical condition caused by faulty genes.

Genetic engineering could reduce the occurrence of such deficiencies. Other inherited diseases, such as sickle cell anaemia and muscular dystrophy, could also be eradicated by altering the genetic code in the parent's eggs or sperm. (This is called germline therapy, discussed in the previous chapter.) It might also be possible to engineer the first fetal cells of an unborn child.

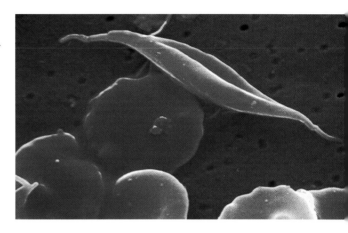

This microscope photograph shows an elongated sickle cell floating among normal red blood cells. Such diseased cells are the result of an inherited illness, passed from parent to child in a faulty gene.

But along with genes for syndromes and diseases, there may also be genes for physical attractiveness, intelligence and personality. As well as offering parents a child free of crippling health problems, genetic engineering presents the possibility of a child designed to have physical traits that its parents believe to be desirable.

Haunted by the past

Hanging over any debate on baby design is the spectre of eugenics – especially the eugenic policy of the Nazis in Germany between 1933 and 1945. In their pursuit of a 'pure-blooded' Aryan race, the Nazis introduced compulsory sterilization of those with physical defects, mental problems, epilepsy, deafness and blindness. The programme was carried out ruthlessly.

Marriages between Germans and so-called 'untermenschen' (sub-humans) such as Blacks, Slavs and Jews were forbidden, and punishable by death. The term used to describe such unions and the children that resulted was 'racial defilement'. But why should the behaviour of a political regime, widely regarded as one of the most evil in recorded history, still influence opinion more than half a century after its collapse?

FACT

Eugenics is the study of methods of improving the quality of the human race. The concept was popular in many countries during the early twentieth century, but is now regarded with great suspicion. This is partly because it attracted the interest of racist regimes such as the Nazis. It is also because human differences are now generally attributed not simply to race, class and gender but to a mix of environmental factors.

Eugenics in action

The most populous nation on Earth, Communist China, has laws concerning human reproduction that citizens in western democracies would find unacceptable. China has a population of over one billion people. One in six people on Earth are Chinese. Because of the problems of housing, feeding and providing work for such a huge population, the Chinese government is attempting to persuade its citizens to have fewer children. There are considerable pressures on, and incentives for, couples to have no more than one or two children. Additionally, there is a great deal of pressure to terminate pregnancies where the baby is thought to be abnormal. Chromosome testing has enabled the government to screen couples who are getting married, and to forbid sexual relations between couples who are likely to pass on inherited diseases.

The crowded streets of Shanghai City, China. The Chinese government is taking drastic action to prevent inherited diseases being passed on to another generation.

Medical advances

In the West, many parents-to-be have medical tests to determine whether a baby the mother carries is going to be healthy. One common test is amniocentesis, where fluid from the womb is checked to indicate the probability of Down's syndrome. There is always a small risk of miscarriage, and accuracy is not guaranteed. The results are not known until over three months into the pregnancy, and the decision on whether or not to terminate what is already a recognizable human being is often a harrowing one.

Genetic screening offers doctors the chance to check genetic defects within days of conception.

This is particularly the case with *in vitro* fertilization (IVF) pregnancies, where the egg is fertilized and begins to divide outside the mother, before being planted in the womb. One test can indicate everything from the sex of the child to the likelihood of it carrying a fatal disease. Such information could be used to indicate cystic fibrosis, Huntingdon's disease, sickle cell disease, Alzheimer's disease, many cancers and even mental illnesses such as schizophrenia. It is also possible to detect defects such as deafness and blindness.

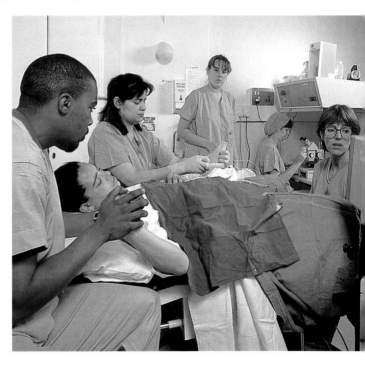

At the moment this knowledge can only be used to help parents decide whether or not they wish to continue with the implantation of the fertilized egg, but in the future it may be possible to correct such characteristics as the fetus grows in the womb.

In vitro fertilization. Patients who conceive in this way can have their fertilized eggs checked for genetic problems before they are replanted in the womb.

Superhuman children

Data from the Human Genome Project will also give parents a window into other characteristics. As we learn to eliminate genetic defects, so too will we learn to enhance positive qualities. HGP research has indicated sets of genes that seem to be responsible for personality types and physical attractiveness. This has led to fears that the ultra-rich will be able to produce superhuman children – superior in intelligence, strength and beauty. Whether this will happen is debatable, but the use of this technology does seem inevitable – just as the advances in safer and more effective surgery this century have led to the huge money-spinning industry of cosmetic surgery.

A doctor carries out an amniocentesis test. In the future, genetic testing will be both safer and quicker.

Nature versus nurture

One American fertility clinic uses genetic screening techniques to offer patients a ninety per cent chance of choosing the sex of their child. But beyond this, there are serious doubts about whether further genetic tinkering will produce the desired results. It might be possible to engineer blue eyes, blond hair and even tallness or slimness, but personality and intelligence are less tangible qualities. Most social scientists agree that ability – whether it be playing the piano well, or getting people to like you – is just as much shaped by environment and experience as by inherited genes. Any parent hoping to buy their child the genes for mathematical genius or a sharp wit may be very disappointed.

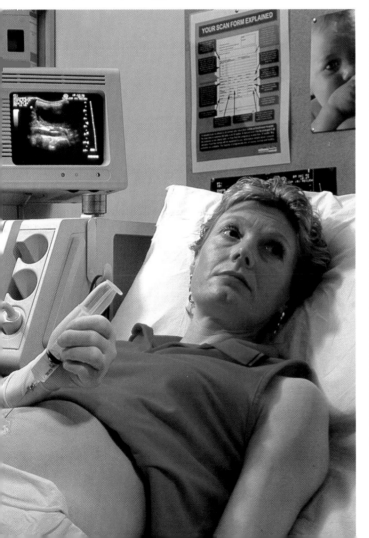

HUMAN CLONING

Evil Twins or Multiple Blessings?

Imagine a world where scientists could duplicate a famous musician or sporting hero, or a where a boy or girl could be reborn if they had died in a childhood accident. This is a world where clones – human replicas – become as commonplace as computers are today. Our ability to make such things happen is just around the corner.

Dolly the sheep was cloned from an ordinary cell, taken from an udder, that had been doctored to grow into a new sheep.

Most people seem to think there is something sinister about this technology, so much so that research into human cloning has been banned in the UK since 1990. But are opponents of this new science like the law-makers who insisted that men with red flags should walk in front of the first motor cars to stop them going too fast, or is there really something dark and dangerous about the business of creating identical human beings?

Science fiction

Cloning has long been a favourite theme of science-fiction cinema and writing, and in most people's minds cloning was as likely to happen as anti-gravity motors, or teleportation chambers. But in February 1997, scientists at the Roslin Institute in Scotland introduced journalists to Dolly the sheep – the world's first mammal cloned from an adult. The news of Dolly's arrival caused a sensation.

Dolly had been created from a single udder cell taken from an adult sheep. The chromosomes in the cell were inserted into another sheep's egg, which had had its own chromosomes removed. The egg was replanted in the sheep it had originally come from, and five months later Dolly was born.

The experiment introduced the world to two major developments in genetic technology:

1. It was possible to produce a complex animal without any kind of sexual reproduction. In other words, the usual process of sperm and egg had been bypassed completely. Any cell from a living organism could be used to do this.

2. A clone would be genetically, and therefore physically, identical to the donor of the original chromosomes.

VIEWPOINTS

'Each human life is unique. I believe we must respect this profound gift and resist the temptation to replicate ourselves.'
President Clinton, on his ban on US government-funded research into human cloning.

'The most upsetting possibility in human cloning isn't superwarriors or dictators. It's that rich people with big egos will clone themselves... So what? Rich and egotistical folks do all sorts of annoying things, and the law is hardly the means with which to try and stop them.'
Nathan Myhrvold, Chief Technology Officer, Microsoft Corporation, USA.

Normal sexual reproduction

Sperm cell containing chromosomes	Egg containing chromosomes	Fertilized egg developing into embryo

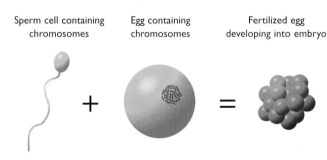

Cloning

Egg with chromosomes removed	Chromosomes from body cell of donor	Developing embryo

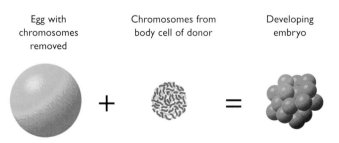

VIEWPOINTS

'Congress should enact a permanent ban on human cloning to keep this frightening idea the province of the mad scientist of science fiction.'
Dick Armey, US congressman.

'Scientists who are interested in cloning aren't mad at all. They want either to help sick people live longer, healthier lives, or to help infertile people have babies.'
James K Glassman, the American Enterprise Institute, 1998.

Sheep to humans

Dolly's arrival pointed boldly to one extraordinary conclusion. If it was possible to clone one type of complex mammal, then it should also be possible to clone a human being. But how likely is it that this will happen?

Currently, cloning is still extremely difficult to achieve. Dolly was the one success in 277 attempts to induce genetic material to develop successfully in a donor egg. Odds like these would make experiments with actual human embryos and surrogate mothers ethically unacceptable. Numerous miscarriages and deformed, barely living babies would cause instant revulsion and outrage among the general public.

But what if public opinion perceived human cloning to be a good thing, and governments decided to invest in research? Some scientists estimate that successful human cloning could be perfected in as few as five years. Research with mice or monkeys, for example, could reveal which adult cells in the body are most suitable for cloning, and the complex process of fusing donor chromosomes and donor eggs could also be improved.

Help for parents?

The most practical, and likely, application for any future cloning technology would be to help infertile couples have their own children. If other conception techniques fail, a couple could opt for a clone child. As with Dolly, an egg from the mother would have its chromosomes removed, and chromosomes from either parent's body cells would be placed inside. The egg could then be replanted in the mother's womb. The technique for this part of the procedure would be very similar to that used in IVF for infertile couples. A child born in this way would then be genetically identical to one of its parents. It would also be that parent's twin brother or sister, but thirty or so years younger.

Why are people so worried about human cloning? Until it is actually done, no one will know how the child or parent will cope with clonehood. Some fear that a parent might expect their child to be just like them, or that a clone child would try desperately to be different and establish its own identity. But this sometimes happens with parents and children anyway. A clone child could not be guaranteed to be just like its parent, as any child is affected by the influences around them, and is not simply a product of their genes.

One unavoidable drawback would be that the child would have much of his or her parent's medical history. Give or take the environmental causes of such conditions, the child would know that he or she would need glasses at the age of sixteen, have grey hair at thirty-five, and develop painful arthritis at sixty. More unpleasantly, if their parent died of cancer at forty-five, the child would know that they too were harbouring a biological time bomb.

VIEWPOINTS

'One of the prospects [of cloning] should not be... the extension of this technique to human beings.... Now that it may be possible, we would say its use should be prohibited if necessary by law.'
Carl Felbaum, President of the Biotechnology Industry Organization, USA.

'Human cloning will not harm people if couples use it to have children they're going to love, and the children are healthy.'
Lee Silver, biologist, Princeton University.

Although it may be possible in theory, there would be little point in producing science fiction clones such as these.

More to come

Looking further into the future, if cloning technology develops at the speed many scientists think it will, all of the following might be possible within the next ten to fifty years:

- The wombs and eggs of large mammals, such as cows, could be used as incubators for donor chromosomes of other mammals, including humans.

- Parents could keep sample body cells of their children. If the child died, the parents could have the cell cloned, and recreate their child.

- People might be cloned without their knowledge. Human skin cells are shed all the time (they make up the major part of household dust), as is human hair. Either could be taken surreptitiously, as they contain the necessary amount of genetic

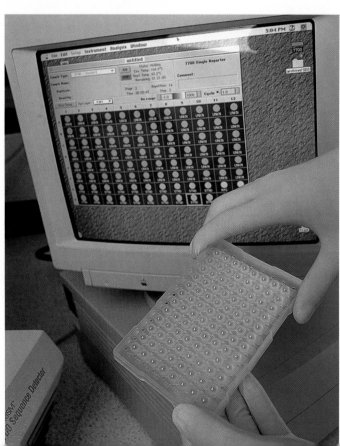

material for cloning. Why would anyone want to do this? Perhaps a rejected partner might want to have a child by their former lover – they could clone their ex-lover's body cells to produce the longed-for baby. Or a totalitarian government might decide that a brilliant athlete or academic should have two (or more) lives to serve his or her nation.

The computer monitor here shows a collection of cloned DNA fragments, used in genetic analysis.

Fatal flaw?

The potential to use this technology for both good and evil is what makes it so unsettling. But scientists working on cloning have another major hurdle to overcome. In May 1999, the company that cloned Dolly the sheep discovered her cells were six years older than her actual age. Dolly came from a sheep who was six. This means that Dolly was effectively six years old when she was born, and may lead a much shorter life than an ordinary sheep.

We shall have to wait and see if this happens, and if it is a characteristic of the cloning process. The idea of bringing a clone baby into the world with a fast-track ageing mechanism would make human cloning a considerably less desirable option.

The idea of human cloning haunts humanity
like no other aspect of genetic engineering.

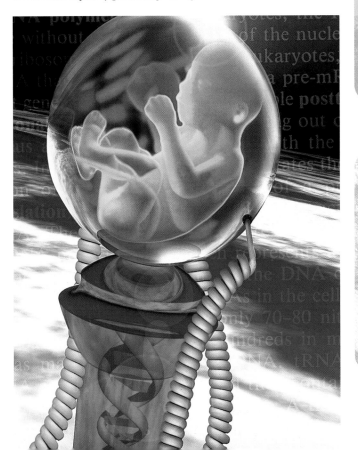

VIEWPOINTS

'I don't think the public wants... families which are distorted because the child is the [genetic] child of only one parent.'
Ruth Deech, Human Fertilization and Embryology Authority, UK.

'What's so special about natural reproduction anyway? Cloning is the only predictable way to reproduce, because it creates an identical twin of a known adult. Sexual reproduction is a crap shoot [a gamble] by comparison – some random mixture of mom and dad....'
Nathan Myhrvold, Chief Technology Officer, Microsoft Corporation, USA.

DEBATE

Today [at considerable expense], a person can have their body frozen when they die. In the distant future, samples of body tissue from such a corpse could be used to create a clone of that person. Do you think this is an acceptable thing to do?

FUTURE DEVELOPMENTS

VIEWPOINTS

'The spectre of nuclear annihilation haunted humanity during the worst days of the Cold War. [Now] we seem poised to risk a different sort of extinction with an altogether different technology. Once again our genius for tinkering with nature is to blame. This time we are not tinkering with the stuff of matter, but the stuff of ourselves.'
US Catholic *magazine article on genetic engineering.*

'Why is it any more plausible to imagine God erecting electric fences around certain areas of knowledge than to imagine God watching with delight and parental pride as human beings use their divinely designed brains to decipher the code of life?'
Chicago Center for Religion and Science, USA.

Breaking barriers, or playing God?

In an ethical world, genetic engineering should be a force for good. Its potential to bring huge benefits to humanity is plain to see. So, is the criticism and suspicion it arouses justified?

The twentieth century has been scarred by the actions of totalitarian regimes of unprecedented brutality. Throughout human history there have been leaders equally as wicked or deluded as Adolf Hitler, Josef Stalin and Mao Zedong, but they lacked the technology that made the regimes of these twentieth-century dictators so powerful. People's fears of genetic engineering are moulded by the knowledge of what humanity is capable of, under the influence of such despotism.

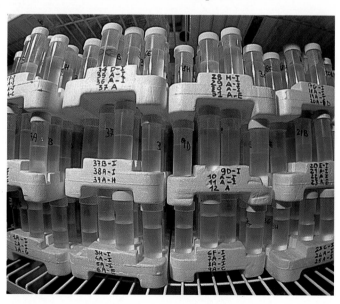

A human gene bank. Genetic material is kept refrigerated in plastic tubes.

Hugely powerful multinational corporations, driven by the desire to maximize their profits rather than any ideological zeal, may be just as potentially destructive. From agribusiness 'terminator seeds' through to patented human genes, there is plenty of scope for human greed to unravel the potential good such technology may bring.

Unknown factors

There are practical problems too. The discovery that Dolly the sheep has body cells that are six years older than her actual age may be a fatal blow to the concept of cloning. But next year, someone may discover a way around this problem. More importantly, do researchers fully understand what they are dealing with? In chromosomes, only three per cent of DNA seems to have any real function.

VIEWPOINT

'In 2003 or 4 the entire human genome sequence will be on the Internet for any nutcase to play with... so watch out folks, it could be a very bumpy ride.'
Dr R E Hurlbert. Washington State University. USA.

If manufacturers can convince their customers that genetically engineered food is a good thing, it may yet become part of everyone's daily diet.

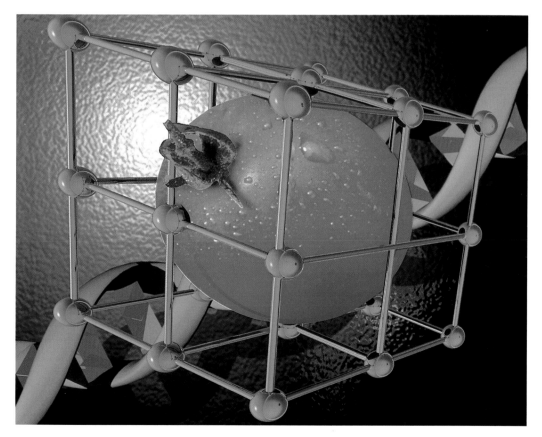

VIEWPOINTS

'Commercial companies are criticized for their involvement in cloning research. But our country earns only twenty-five per cent of its wealth from manufacturing. In future we shall live increasingly on brains, not brawn.'
Professor Robert Winston. Professor of Fertility Studies. Hammersmith Hospital. London.

'My worry is that other advances in science may result in other means of mass destruction, maybe more readily available than nuclear weapons. Genetic engineering is quite a possible area, because of these dreadful developments that are taking place there.'
Joseph Rotblat. 1995 Nobel prize physicist, on bioweapons.

The other ninety-seven per cent is something of a mystery. How this ninety-seven per cent affects the important three per cent, we don't yet know. The way in which new combinations of genes act on other genes is also very poorly understood. These factors may affect the outcome of research in a way that is impossible to predict.

New breakthroughs

Genetic engineering is a very young science. It has developed at extraordinary speed. Every day, it seems, there are new breakthroughs. Many advances in technology arouse deep suspicion. The first heart transplant and the first successful IVF 'test-tube baby' were greeted with cries of 'crime against nature' and 'playing god'. But today most people find medical procedures such as these perfectly acceptable.

This scientist is part of a team who have discovered that obesity is linked to a gene that regulates our appetite.

In June 2000 the leading private genetic research company Celera Genomics, and the publicly funded Human Genome Project, made a joint declaration. They announced that between them they had decoded ninety per cent of the human genome and agreed to publish a joint rough draft of this. Behind the announcement lay a bitter feud about who should own this information. The Human Genome Project remains committed to making this data freely available. Celera Genomics want to sell sections of the code which they have discovered to pharmaceutical companies. How this issue is resolved could have a profound effect on the use of this extraordinary new technology.

DEBATE

One American fertility clinic uses genetic screening techniques to offer patients a ninety per cent chance of choosing the sex of the child they want. Should parents be allowed to choose the sex of their child?

Genetically engineered seeds may provide future farmers with better protected and more plentiful crops.

GLOSSARY

allergen a substance which causes an allergy.

allergy an unfavourable reaction in the body to a particular substance.

antibiotic a drug that kills harmful bacteria.

bacteria single-cell organisms, many of which cause disease.

cells tiny building blocks that make up plants and animals.

chromosome a strand of DNA containing genes.

cloning the process of creating cells or living things with identical DNA.

DNA deoxyribonucleic acid – a nucleic acid which makes up genes.

embryo an animal in the first stages of development from a fertilized egg.

enzyme a chemical process which speeds up life processes, such as digestion, in living things.

evolution a gradual change in the characteristics of a species.

fossil fuels coal, gas and oil.

gene a length of DNA which confers a specific characteristic to an individual.

herbicide a chemical used to kill weeds.

immunity the ability of a living thing to resist disease.

molecule a group of atoms which are bonded together.

multinational a business organization which operates in several countries or continents.

nucleus the part of the cell which controls its activity and contains genetic material.

organism any living plant or animal.

pathogen any micro-organism which causes disease.

pesticide a chemical used to kill insects which eat plants.

raw material any natural material used in a manufacturing process.

resistance a body's ability to fight disease.

skin graft surgery involving the replacement of damaged skin with new skin.

syndrome a combination of signs and symptoms which indicate a disease or disorder.

totalitarian state an oppressive, one-party regime.

toxins poisonous substances produced in the body by micro-organisms.

virus a micro-organism that can only reproduce by invading a living cell.

ACKNOWLEDGEMENTS

Students may find the following books useful:

Genetic Engineering (Moral Dilemmas series), Sally Morgan, Evans (London) 1998.

In the Blood: God, Genes and Destiny, Steve Jones, Flamingo (London) 1996.

Sexing the Parrot: Changing the World with DNA, Dr Wilson Wall, Cassell (London) 1999.

The Language of Genes, Steve Jones, Flamingo (London) 1994.

The ideas expressed in this book came from hundreds of websites, and many recent newspapers and also from television news or documentary programmes. The author would particularly like to acknowledge the following:

Redesigning the World: Ethical Questions about Genetic Engineering by Ron Epstein, lecturer, Philosophy Department, San Franscisco State University, USA. http://userwww.sfsu.edu/~rone/gedanger.htm

Biotech Buccaneers by Monte Paulsen, *Fairfield County Weekly*, 1998. http://www.fairfieldweekly.com

Double Jeopardy by Tim Radford in *The Guardian*, 23 May 1998.

The Seeds of Wrath by John Vidal in *The Guardian*, 19 June 1999.

The Bioweaponeers by Richard Preston in the *New Yorker*, 9 March 1998.

The Babymakers, broadcast in the UK on Channel 4, October 1999.

Curing the Incurable, broadcast in the UK on Channel 4, October 1999.

Newsnight, a discussion chaired by Kirsty Wark on civil liberty issues arising from genetic databases, broadcast in the UK on BBC2, September 1999. The quotes in chapter five by Tom Shakespeare, Dr Karl Stefansson, Dr Richard Nicholson and Dr Einar Arnason are taken directly from this programme. Comments made by Dr Richard Nicholson and Dr Karl Stefansson during this discussion are also quoted in chapter six.

USEFUL ADDRESSES

You may like to access the websites of the following institutions
for research material for genetics-related projects.

The Australian Biotechnology Association
http://www.aba.asn.au

The British Nutritional Foundation
http://www.nutrition.org.uk

European Federation of Biotechnology
http://sci.mond.org/efb

Green Alliance
http://www.green-alliance.demon.co.uk

Greenpeace International
http://www.greenpeace.org

The Human Genome Project
http://www.ornl.gov/hgmis

Monsanto
http://www.monsanto.com

**The National Centre for Biotechnology
Education, AMS**
http://www.ncbe.reading.ac.uk

**The National Museum of Science
and Industry**
http://www.nmsi.ac.uk

Novartis
http://www.novartis.com

**The United States Food and
Drugs Administration**
http://www.FoodSafety.gov

INDEX